Lake Nora Arms

Lake Nora Arms

MICHAEL REDHILL

To Lynn —
in friendship
& with admiration.
Love,
Michael

COACH HOUSE PRESS
TORONTO

Published with the assistance of the Canada Council,
the Department of Communications, the Ontario Arts
Council and the Ontario Publishing Centre.

Canadian Cataloguing in Publication Data

Redhill, Michael, 1966–
    Lake Nora Arms

Poems.
ISBN 0-88910-460-3

I. Title.

PS8585.E34L3 1993   C811'.54   C93-094679-0
PR9199.3.R44L3 1993

For Ted Cadsby and Tim Singh

And in memory of Robert Sklar

No, perdóname.
Si tú no vives,
Si tú, querida, amor mío,
si tú
te has muerto,
todas las hojas caerán en mi pecho,
lloverá sobre mi alma noche y día ...

No, forgive me.
If you are not living,
if you, beloved, my love,
if you
have died,
all the leaves will fall on my breast,
it will rain on my soul, all night, all day ...

— Pablo Neruda

YOU ARE HERE

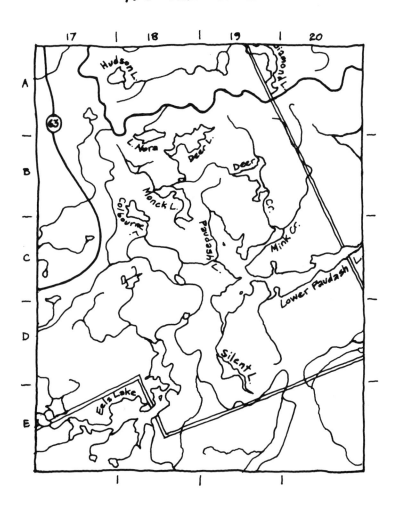

I want to sleep in Lake Nora Arms. On your shoulder, beside you, the scent of diesel coming in through a window. Old men in alleys nearby. I want to soak a velour towel with us and wake with my mouth still drunk on you. Lake Nora Arms. Long stairwell. Blue hallways. Killers rented out rooms there. Bullets in the chambers. Dillinger stayed in one, maybe, with a single sunrise reserved for his pleasure. I want that sunrise, want the place his brain went. Hoover killed him. Now Hoover's dead. Now Hoover's dead. He killed him.

Be eighteen again and in Lake Nora Arms. I could take you to the Runcible Spoon and drink the worst iced tea in the whole of the Great Canadian Shield, in the Runcible Spoon, with you, reading their socially correct posters: *Save the red muskrat, Save the ermine.* Save the iced tea, it was a great place. You had long fingernails and you painted them the colour of your fingers. On the way back, depending on the night, people would throw us Michelobs from their balconies. It was good to drink beer on hot nights. We could tell stories the whole night, all the details intact. Then we'd have to sleep on top of the sheets, our pores clogged with drink, our wet skin, our sheets, the moon beating down. Or we'd drag a blanket to the park and sleep beneath a tree, while all around us punks on skateboards. Or muscular women.

I want to walk to Big Wheel and bring back waffles and Coke to Lake Nora Arms. Eat Wint O Green and pass it back and forth in our mouths, until the little pellet is gone. Stay up late in Lake Nora Arms and admit secrets. I watched a friend's parents make love when I was in grade three. You had an abortion when you were seventeen. The doctor held your face in his hands and whispered in your ear: *Diamond in the rough.* You had a rubber clamp in your mouth. The walls were thin as paper there. We could keep our secrets, but not how we felt about them. Arguments and orgasms drifted through the walls. Screams, grunts, shouts followed by laughter. Lake Nora Arms.

I would cut my toenails with the television on, and when you came out of the bathroom, there would be a cloud of steam flowing behind you like a dress. I would come and hold you, be wed for a moment in a disappearing cloud. While you sleep, I want to watch the cars drift by, their high-beams sweeping out along an empty road, the drivers counting off exits like chapters before the highway starts again. Cows would low with longing in their voices, stricken by moon-light. I would come in my sleep beside you and wake beside you in my sleep. If only I could walk into the photographs of Lake Nora Arms before they tore it down, open the cupboards and discover the history of paint-jobs, greet the travelling salesmen with their samples akimbo at their feet. I want to feel and turn a corner and turning the corner, see it all living again.

I could meet the manager in his yellow tie, who told you his cock bent to the left and you told him mine did too, and he was nicer to me after that. I could smell the hair of women at breakfast, eat the eggs as they slid around in their butter, salt an apple, stare at the van Gogh haystacks on the wall. You could lean across the table and tell me you hated your mother. Then decide what to do for the day. A fly would land in the jam. Lake Nora Arms nine o'clock Lake Nora Arms.

If I was back at Lake Nora Arms, we could watch the football game in our room, then look out the window to the field and watch our friends tear out the goalposts and parade them through town. I would walk with you later, the runcinate leaves in the air, the air cool, the cool earth. We could watch the man in the black vest climb his ladder and change the name of the film. He would truncate it until we were weak with laughter. He would shorten it until there was nothing left to recall and no picture it could make. In Lake Nora Arms I could look at the ceiling all night, feel your skin and never tire of it. All around us, the whizzing of bullets started with a low hum in the dreams of loners. Elderly women placed calls into the past to dead girlfriends and lovers. There was always

trouble and unhappiness next door, always set-
backs, one-legged men falling over in the hall-
way. I want to stand in the darkened stairwell
of Lake Nora Arms, darkened and me inside it
with your scent there, walk the halls and come
back to you, step into love beside your body
silent as the end of a name, your blue gown
your night sky, your breath smooth as the
sound of a train far off beyond town, moving
slow as a dream, its country shifting like a
dream. I want to sleep in Lake Nora Arms.
Lake Nora Arms.

Cars doppler outside

The Story of Water

is told from parent to child
its tributaries twisting
in the mind. *Remember water?*
someone says. Yes
I remember water.

> *I first saw water*
> *fading at a party, lonely*
> *in the kitchen. It was*
> *listening to us as we argued.*
> *Water wanted*
> *to clear everything up between us.*

When I kiss you now, water
is the hidden part under your tongue—
you but not quite you, water
in the middle of transformation.

It has the slow mind of a killer,
protean, stupid, dangerous. It held
a boy I knew too tight. Water
is inside us, its mind
crusted with salt.

What I want is water

to keep us suspended like this.
Being everywhere, water
is in our thoughts. My desire for you
drifts under the brain's ocean.

Water claimed so many of us,
our attraction to it was
pure addiction. Water
laughed it off, saying
HOH HOH HOH.

We'll never get to the bottom of it.

In the Arms

At dusk, old men fresh from the city
gathered for drinks and the laughter rose
in stages like a rocket—such a lonely time
for kids. I remember it—as a child
I carved my name on trees, was called in
for suppers, sunblock, aurorae boreales.

Thinking about it makes the walls rise up,
those old tables and secret places. I am standing
in the late-night halls, with faces that float
like coins in the air, the childless couples passing
on the way to their rooms. Or is this dark space
the little chamber where a sick child slept,
a not unfrightening fever going, the glowing night light
so promising in the corner? Later we all returned,
with our loves, or marriages at an end
and had our silent days, sitting with books and tea,
the lake-watching window
laying our eyes in the trees.

That window, framed in wood,
rolled the moon like a marble
in its arch. Wrapped in blankets,
as child or adult lovers, we heard
voices say *is everything up there named?*
and *I'm still afraid of the dark.*

One Year

Was that you cocooned
in his father's hammock or perched on end
of branch, dangling, spiderlike, afraid?
Hard to recall—we were boys,
those tricks were brave, pranks we played
at the feet of death. To fall or unwind meant loss—
of breath at least—that was pretty scary.
(If temporary.) We knew we'd somehow last.
In cold rain we'd go missing, vanish
into slick canoes and go on kissing hunts
to friends across the lake, dive in lilac
or brackish water, watch the backs of fish
curved like lashes swimming—was that you?
If I have you in the right place,
that's your face there sitting in Napoli's
eating pizza, putting your mother at unease
staining your summer pants—*Please
be more careful!* Boys can get into trouble:
they could see us in the dusk on the lake,
motor cut, gliding into fog, or that hognosed
snake that burrowed in dust that we found
was poisonous. All these things we survived.
And to think now how easily I left you
when one of us had had enough—*I'm not ready yet,
I'll meet you inside*—and I had
stayed out a while and played. I think

it's true then—you've actually died.
If this is you (and you've gone missing
if it's not) I want to tell you
I'm still angry, and I think of you a lot.

The Runcible Spoon

You look up from your book
where the great Pelé plays his last game.
He cries to the crowd
Love! Love! Love!
I want you to say it with me!
I sip my iced tea and ask you
to ask him to keep it down. I'm trying
to get a perspective on Cubism.
We've been here all afternoon with books,
shutting out the noise,
watching each other read. We argue
a small point: Did Leopold Kessler
blow up that train? I argue Cubistically
—yes and no—you argue like Pelé,
run circles around me. Our books live
brief lives within us while all around
we hear quick moral emergencies:
You could make it if the airliner crashed
and you survived by eating a few friends.
You carry those you love inside you forever.
Can you imagine
terror at the controls, the 747
going down, and the man who moments earlier
had explained glacial striation
—see those fingerlike lakes—
is crying on your shoulder?

You're still trying to read. Then just say it
with me: Love! Love! Love!
We will have to eat it to live.

What Separates Us

This street scene, for one.
You can't see the lake, scrap
book city—they pasted the pictures
too close together. Underneath,
all that space where we
tabled our desire
and it grew.

Strange. After supper
we rebuilt the chicken
and found teeth and a huge legbone.
What evolved in death? We should
leave it be what it was
starting to become. We ate
that thing and it became us. Strange

bodies all over. In my bed
we are twined, yet our talons
leave almost no marks. By morning
they have gone. You remember
an aerial dream (sexual), I
dreamt of Buicks, which is the way
Dream says *eagle*. Somehow
we will remain together.

Which is more than I can say
for myself. I stand naked in my house
at the window, search my mind
for food. Stretched

outside, the telephone wires
that connect the trees.
Now the trees become
our tongues, they rebuild us,
manage our grammar,
click and moan.

But their alphabet
is broken at their feet.

I Am Ruminating Over You

for my friend, Jon

9:00	Rise
9:15	Ratatouille
9:25	Shwarma
9:45	Soursop
10:15	Tarragon grilled fish
10:45	Capers
11:20	Petits fours
12:00	Mutton in mint
12:35	Falafel
1:00	Lunch
1:45	Reuben
2:15	Trifle
3:00	Trifle
3:15	Pickled eggs
4:00	Soda bread
4:15	Beef tongue
4:45	Tom ka kai
5:00	Lime Jell-o
6:15	Head cheese
6:35	Hors d'oeuvres
6:40	Dinner
7:15	Lemons
8:00	Swordfish Dijonnaise
8:30	Lavender tea
8:45	Tomato, bocconcini and garbanzos

9:20	Apple/cranberry fruit leather
9:45	Chutney buttock
10:30	Iced coffee
10:50	Broth
11:00	Almond wafer
11:15	Bacon and cheese perogies with sour cream
11:25	Bed

Eighth Floor, Room 710

I work at a law firm and you know
my supervisor, he came down
and he say "we better make a work plan
for you, Jenny," and you know
what he said, he said "sexsexsex"
do you think he was insulting me?
Do you think he was trying to tell me
a insult? I am not a whore!
But what can you do?
Is this crazy or what? My father
was a fucking bastard you know
so blame it all on him, you know
he go into a room and when he come out
guess what? All these little men
are with him. What do you think?
My father make all those little men?
My father tell them to go out
and find me later? I am not a whore
you hear that? They all touchtouchtouch
oh my, say "hey, no problem
Jenny," just like that and touch me
on the cunt. Do you think
I am lying? I should get
out of here, what do you think?
This fucking city, all I see is
lesbian nuns and devil doctors.

Are you treating me nice? I can find you
if maybe you are laughing at me
or writing every word I say down
because you think I am crazy.
I work at a law firm and you know

Clara M: A Case History

I dream of Clara M.
She tells me eating
is a nuisance to her.
She eats herself.
I am standing in a church with her
and she delivers a sermon from the pulpit
in my father's cloak. Clara's mouth
speaks a tongue of dangerous intent.
Then the scene shifts. We are in my office.
    Clara sits in the leather chair
behind my desk and anoints herself
with balm of Gilead.
Perhaps Clara is deeper in her illness
than I thought. I elect to have her placed
in the white room for a week. She will be calm.
I speak with H. He thinks she is in *doppelgänger*
transference. This is why she appears in my dreams
as men. I do not love Clara M.
    Clara is showing me her genitals.
I cannot repeat her unpleasant offer.
I suggest I will be forced to leave
unless she covers up. Clara M.
does not wish to be abandoned.
Later I dream a snake with her face
emerges from that dark place.
Note to myself: the snake

is a hero archetype. I spend
the evening after dinner in the rock garden.

My wife has made love to me
furiously. I do not understand
this force that emerges.
The skin gives off a muddy energy.
I must bring the instruments home,
I must part that mystery in the middle.
At an early hour, I awaken.
I stand at the window and watch the sun
rise in the oily sky. My face
is draining in its direction.

I am burning. I am burning
at the centre of my being.
Clara is beyond my help.
I do not understand her. My dreams
have gone silent. Clara:
all hope is gone, I have failed.
My love, my only one,
my broken-hearted prince-woman.

I have stopped dreaming of Clara M.
I am empty of her deviances. I am
clean. It is strange: I do not see her
ever. Not on the street, not in the cafés.
My wife is well; my boys are strong-limbed.
Yes. I am young and full of life.

Tilted in from the hallway, eyes quick: Joanne

She spreads her hands wide,
sits in my chair
and the room bends in
like a spotlight.

She lowers her head.
Something thrashes behind her eyes,
Julian's angry body, her memory
of pills. How he took them,
crazy Julian wanting his way.

I see them as they were,
never happy. And now,
how his insides must be opening
like a zipper with the poison,
like a welt forming
between the organs, the
plastic cases popping open
and spreading like a sunset.

Her hands cover her face,
the moons on her fingernails
gibbous, the moons
coming up from dark.

(Four miles away,
they attach him
like a kite to the machines.)

Bliss

A Christmas party—cheers—ginger-snap,
fizzy punch. Someone
is telling me I'm breathing in a molecule
of Napoleon's nose with every breath. Thank you.
Do we know anyone else here?

So many years ago. That year
Christ died again and all our friends
went on living. Amazing—
this belief still waving around
like a room full of smoke.

What I believe is I'll have another drink.
I have faith there will come a day
when I will be animal again
and everything that is sensual
will be sacrament.

I'll breathe you in off an old sweater,
out of a photo. Memory
makes you rise. I wish
we went back to a time
when we understood nothing,
when people
weren't exterminating themselves.

Young Loves

In the Sunday café
they gather shy as ghosts,
still stunned from sex.
They're arranged in twos and fours
strange serenities etched
on their faces. Young wives
with their strong bodies take tea
and ease conversation around,
touch their husbands and smile.
At home the men are still in the habit
of cooking dinner and there are pauses
in everything for sex. They feel
their bodies are out on loan. The men
walk behind the women and it's confirmed:
no one knows what the hell's going on,
but it's lovely, anyway.
When will unhappiness strike?
Who will be the first
to awaken in bed and feel alone?
Soon they will have to love each other
in the impermanence of what awaits them
and that will be difficult, that time
which life pays you for in advance.

Euridice at Yonge and Bloor

How long have you been gone?
In the subway,
I sense you behind me
on the escalator. The smell
of morning coffee is all around.
Train riders pass me, the cold street
streaming off their coats.
Some mornings you would say
Don't look at me—
I'm not up yet. And now
knowing to be with you again
means resisting my heart.
I let little bits of you
take shape in the air.
To see without looking
is a lover's art.

Out

A sun is under those fields.
Comes up yellow. Drive.
City wavelengths follow us,
and splinter in the radio.
Music on the tape deck now.
She's asleep, sweater bunched up.
Door locked? Can't see.
Simcoe. Fishing's cruel she thinks.
I used to like it, six a.m. with my dad,
purple-grey dawn, rice crackers.
Worm smell. Here's a sign:
400 kilometres to—GLARE—
we could get lost like this
driving into the sun. Love her hair,
saffron. Nice houses. Cottages?
How can we say we've been here?
Just driving past, looking out
this is my country (I've seen it
from cars and trains). We're
going through it. Want to stop the car
and watch her sleep. Look:
she's there, all of her, in this car!
Animal asleep. Headlights on now.
Semaphore: we drive—

              Where are we?

                          Simcoe.

Deep blue mosaic

Perishable

Undulating at a safe remove
the object of our desire
split open like a zipper at three a.m.
and left us gaping at it, left us

reeling at the sweet odour. I know
it is too easy to reproach
oneself for slight blunders,
but nothing had prepared us for this,

this jelly, which throbbed fitfully
and seemed to reach out to us. This
was not a God, or a projection of it,
but rather what our science

had conjured and our art defined, creator
and created, the homunculus
cleft from our souls and skin. It was sweet
at first; they played Rachmaninoff

as they unveiled it. The sound
of a weeping piano
warbled over the P.A.
The cheesecloth was dripping

as the men brought it past us.
We began to move closer to it—
jostling each other, our
collective heart pounding. I was the first

at its side. I could not have predicted
it would have howled like a sick infant,
or lay there stunned and quivering
unable to do what we'd designed it for.

Listen

You can hear in here the lapping
long and low against your sleeping shore.

At the bottom of all air it's there
at the bottom of all breath you take it in.

Why haven't you heard Lake Nora?

Dram of a dream.

True Story

You got your big lakes and you got your small lakes.
From space it looks like a buckshot stopsign.
Some of 'em are knee-deep all the way across
(like your Nipissing)
and these ones breed your giant insatiable pike.
A friend of mine let his golden
jump around in the water, way up see,
and the dog could swim, but then suddenly
it vanishes. "Ranger!" we're yelling,
"Ranger!" But Ranger doesn't answer.
Pike attack. Honest.
Now you listen to me:
Don't walk across Lake Nipissing—
run. Run like hell because they got pike in that lake.

How To Find Lake Nora

The earliest map in the Arms is dated 1899. The quilted land-scape is dotted with huge spills: Muskoka, Joseph, Rosseau. Lake Nora is at B18, nestled in the word WOOD, the name of the county it lies in. All the names are taken from the early colonists of the forests. Medora. Monk. Humphrey. Wood. And the lakes are named for the fallen: beaver, deer, pigeon, loon. Among the early settlers we find Reverend Bland at B12 in a small hut where he made his own syrups and went mad in 1911. And at G22, the Cartwright summer home. Cartwright, the true conquering spirit. He sat in his chilly front room win-ter after winter with only a single candle, and watched his face float in that harsh light reflected against the window, saw his eyes rise disembodied over the trees. Cartwright rubbed his hands to keep them warm, and to feel less anxious and alone. But he was fearful. He had found Lake Nora.

To find Lake Nora, think about the shore of Couchiching. Ride the thought through the Severn locks, past the sanatorium at C48, marked in block letters at the bottom of the map. Lake Nora whistles through these places to her throne, dragging the graphed lines with her like a thrashing salmon breaking through the net. Lake Nora is ready for battle when she gets there, dispatching chiding red squirrels and magpies down the chimney.

To find Lake Nora go Sherpa. Stop looking. Read the signs. To find Lake Nora follow the signal in your teeth. To find Lake Nora, return all your library books, believe in nothing.

To find me surrender.

Lake Nora Quartet

i

In Toronto, the dead lie in clusters
at intersections. The trees shade
the roofs of cars, the sun
lights up the stones: BYRD,
MANN. One hundred miles to the north,
in the town of my birth, the dead
lie soft as timber, and the sun
cannot reach them because my heart
is so far down. Particle armies
hanging in my body drink the light
and down below in the silt
lie the mouldering boaters.

ii

Bell telephone is here.
They've wired the frontier.

Looo loo loo loooooooo
Kit-deee kit-deee kit-deee
Drrrrrringggg drrrringgg drrrringgg.

iii

The pike swung against the line
and pulled. The hook tore into its mouth
and locked. It leapt out of the water
and saw its reflection hurled against the sky.
It was a very big fish. It was a good fish.
Nick tugged on the line and reeled it in.

That's what ya get ya goddam fish
fer chewing the legs offa my dog!

iv

I slow down when it rains on Lake Nora.
I watch it fall from inside a window.
The rain can make you feel like someone's said
things were different then.
The lake jumps up all over.

Three Ships

i

I wish I could write a chapter upon sleep—
then all these dreamers could converge,
the pleasure-boaters, ginned and sunburnt,
the wooden canoes with the children in their boxy
red life-jackets, waiting. The docks
lie like fingers along the shoreline,
holding the water down taut as Cellophane.

Then a heron takes off, chewing the air.
Behind it the prow of a giant ship
rises frothing out of the water wild.
The little boats rock. We can see
the children suddenly reach around them.
Air pockets from the ship explode
like divers gasping, and we're waving
from the windows—

Wake up now!

ii

I'm sitting in the marsh at six a.m.
The outboard scared the shorebirds.
Now they begin to ease back, hungry
for the fish blood in the water. Where I go
there's food. I'm danger and opportunity.

iii

The next thing never happens
and the ship vanishes.
What's under there can't see them.
They scatter like minnows in their boats,
then regroup. They're somehow
both wide awake and asleep.

Lake Nora as a Woman in a Plummeting Airliner

Sadness. I mothered splintered millions,
but I am barren. I sit
and watch the sky get caught in my face
over and over. I am barren. An old man
his hair in wisps sits alone, watching
the space in front of him grow smaller.
I want to take his hand as we fall, want him
not to be alone. He reminds me
of my father, who is dead, sifted back
in time. I had wished to be beautiful
for him. I hold back out of fear.

I hold this man as the sky
speeds up in the surface of a cousin
who rises into my window. Childless,
so he has taken the names of mine to speak
as we enter the lake: bulrush, brown trout,
leopard frog, snake. They will never find my body.
Mother you have made all things one being.
I hold this man who bears my children
on his lips. So I hold myself
and I vanish.

Lake Nora as the Golem

I walk in the darkness
and leave a silvery trail.
The sign on my forehead
(B18) is the beacon
that draws me deeper into the scene.

Protector and fiend,
I gobble tykes on bikes
and thump the hollow streets
with my tail. Under the pavement
my sisters slide in runnels of gloom
and pop up in toilets
and sitting-rooms.

I am lonely though and miss
my fa. His hands were cool
on my face. And now, I have to walk
freezing in my shoes
all night in this filthy place!

If I had a mouth I would howl!
If I had eyes I would cry!

But I have nothing
but this black mud whorled into skin.
And this fear that I'm going to die.

Gardener's Shed

The implements hung hooked there
in shadows, iron hands
grasping peat, the smell of pine, jar-lined
shelves with bolts and screws,
and nails dormant as bullets
in their cans.

Each late June the trellises
went up, bean ladders, coils
for voluptuary fruits. Zucchini leaves
webbed and pale as frog feet
spread a green realm. The gardener
stood there under a rainy moon.
Go home and love your wife!

But the gardener hears the shower
spackling the roof of his tin house.
The doors scrape open, and a young boy sees
the barrow and a man's white hair:
the gardener's shed splitting like a pod,
the old man's head as if bent in prayer.

Fallow Watch

The shovel chips the cherry dark
smashing the roots where electricity
sparks. And there, gleaming and fogged
some of the roots have grown watch-faces.
The gardener leans in and changes the batteries,
lifts the clods back into place.

The alarms have been set.
In six months the buzzing will begin
and the green and white cases will stretch and tune in
like crusty-eyed boys and girls in their rooms
starting to fill in, fill out, thicken and bloom.

Spring Planting

Olive forehead behind the *New York Times,* time to go
time to go he's late sharp Armani cut hides
boyish shoulders glass of coffee tilted
as he reads. Water glass with the microbe
frosts at his elbow time to go he gulps
the glassy ice and the hairy character floating.

Retroboosting microphage angles down into soft loam
pinky countryside and the hooks are buried and herald
spores float out like newsboys. He rushes out the door
it's all beginning little insurrection as he
hails the cab and talks trade talk with the driver
as he thinks of his lover, his Tina, his great reason

she's stopped loving him and waving in the villi
are little electrical impulses that are like
photographs of her floating down a river. All day
he sprouts behind his desk rising and lowering
according to rank and as he sits, sits rising
and lowering something in its tiny partitions

is thundering upwards, filaments branching in hospitable
nooks hair growing up inside him *Salis Staphylococcus,*
Betula Plasmodium and a bell is ringing: four a.m.
something in his head goes off throat is like a hypo
he gets out of bed crashing limps to the mirror
hearing the hissing slap of his feet moist on tile

and in the mirror, the jack pine busting his head.

Signature

As a boy he had carved
his name into the acacia.
The tree built around the scar of his name,
spreading it, worrying it smooth.

Time elides this word like Old-World names.

A puncture on his hand spreads out too,
ridges of skin dissolving in waves,
skin lapping onto a shore of skin

as if a stone has been thrown
into the lake of his body.

*

A tree against the sun is an arm shielding an eye.

Under their skins, trees ripple out.

The seed tossed in earth rings up through the trunk.

This page was year sixty-three.

Time is buried in the rings.

Tongues are laced in the green wood.

A tree is an arm up against the arm of a man.

YOU ARE HERE

Lake nora arms lake nora arms

The Splinter

Strata of skin, a fisted forest
grows inside a hand. Its thin
black shape vanishes like fishing-line
into a lake. It comes out
with a pearl of blood,
leaves a scar or story.
In seven years the mark will vanish,
the body's cycle complete.
The dash of wood gets tossed in the lake,
floats then sinks. Cup water
in the wounded hand and drink:
taste iron. The sand
covers up the splinter
at the bottom of the water.

Phases

Ich glaube an Nächte

Watching the garden winter under the moon,
we think of the brown animals
under the earth. Or the bulbs
of the jonquils frozen there
with their orange eyes clenched in coils.
White and silent night, the air cold as iron
and the lake like an old woman under a blanket.
We gave your grandma marijuana tea
to lull the cancer clenched in her like fists.

Our legs are weak after making love
but we walk across the solid lake.
We're wrapped in the husk of a Bay blanket,
the air smells like wool and our heat
billows around us, animal. The lake
clicks as we walk, a photograph
curling up at the edges. Far under,
hibernating fish drift in the current,
their bodies curving back and forth,
while above them the moon
glows on the snowless patches—
a white heart expanding under the ice.
And in our blanket, our bodies
hold the shapes of the people
whose cells we slept in for generations.

Intermarriage

A secret dinner, away from our lives.
We set the table, do not sense
the ten o'clock darkness outside
although we are joined to it.

Beyond the blinds, the moon
is rusting the lake.
　　　Love the right things.

This abundance disappoints me.
My mouth needs the lingering
tang of skin,
sprigs of hair,
buds, tendrils, blooms—
the earth of the body,
moon-breast, finger-on-the-lip.

Why can't we be joined in a garden
where the congregants
stand dumb in the earth?

Bedtime Haiku

Dual pools of light, we're
reading our books silently.
Cars doppler outside.

And then you drift off—
such a sad foreknowledge. I
wish you'd keep reading.

The Physical World

I have slept on your shoulder
sweat flowering out in lines
as you sleep, transforming you.
Our human shape dissolves,
we are bees, are pitcher-plants
with insects struggling within us,
are children again, shame
deserting us. I taste your arms,
the salt an electric charge running
from your skin into my mouth.
You have been dreaming of onions.
I can taste it. Nothing separates us
but everything keeps us apart.

Underground

The red worms darted out of our light,
displacing the moon on leaves they touched.

We walked deeper into the brown field—
nothing close to us was moving, but

distant leaf tips tilted up and down:
a sinister sound that kept stopping.

We stood still and turned off the light.
The noise grew—it was a sound that came

from underground. We knew
that from their wet loam they saw us,

and we were in a place they thought
was under. *I think we should go back*—

but we had waited too long and now,
all the way out, their red bodies

were lacing the air wild as vines.
The whole field was a muscle beneath us.

Sing

The first drunk was the worst:
a blend of cassis and Jack Daniel's,
anything that wouldn't be missed.
Fifteen years old, holding hands and howling
up the street in our underwear.
We recorded it all on tape,
the one with the sound of your barfing,
the one you think I've lost.
Years later, our voices are muffled
our mouths casting about for words.
I can hear you singing
remember me forever...

Even though we said years
would not pass, they did. Perhaps
we became foolish men (like
some of our friends). Now
you live very far from me
and I long for you
as if I were still a boy.
If you would call me
I could try to make it like it was,
and one of us would unburden the day
and say "enough?" and the other
"keep going." And after

end up at one or the other's house
easily unwinding the mysteries
that bind us now.

I still listen for things
we'd both like, tunes
we might do one day, the way
we sat at your piano
savaging the Greats, laughing
and swearing at my terrible voice.
You'd only swear by saying "Brother!"
—an oath said with a certain kind of knowing.
And now my oath is this note to you,
"Enough?" it says.
        "Keep going."

Nightfall

The boat drives past the island cottage locked
in its privacy. Night falls on the lake.
You and I, drowsed with dusk, slowly talk
the darkness down and watch a gliding drake
dislodge the clouds around our boat and crack
the sky below us. In this clear weather
the stars seem to brighten for our sake—
they appear like berries on the lake
glowing near the boat, close enough to gather.

Deck Building

The long summer it went up
nail by nail—difficult
to reconstruct. The once huge days
clench into hours of the mind,
the pictures splintered, moving
tongue and groove into each other.
Here, a hammock and a line of berries
budding. Here, a mother
rescuing cold children from a lake
into towels, rubbing heat
into their bellies. I see my
purpled fingers in her hand,
her breath warming them.

Those summers the cottage grew
in increments like our bodies.
New shingles, stripped wood,
front room, a deck. My father and I
built it from pine and cedar.
The sap glued our hands to the wood.
His back when he worked
was spotted with pearls.
Beer nearby, its salty edge
on my tongue. I'm twelve,
big enough to share a beer.
As we hammer and fit

the dogs chase squirrels. Beautiful
dogs, prisoners of summer.
I feel the hammer blows
up my arms, the satisfying
force that slides the nail in,
its narrow sound.
We create a false earth. Flat
as the sky looks, knocking each plank
into place, lining them up
like bean rows. The imagined
night-drinkers appear
as ghosts in my mind. I see them
walking on the pieces
we put together.

By the end of the summer, we were
staining it, and when it was finished
he stood out on it, alone with his thoughts,
still, like a tree. I watched him
from the window, seeing how he saw
his world grow up around him
and although I could feel his thoughts
I didn't know what they were.

A Room in Winter

Not the way it is now, the way it was
with us framed in a ghosted window.
You lay in the day-bed clueless with fever,
I was armed with hot water,
two tiny teacups—death repelled
by ceremonies. Because you couldn't speak
we had silence. You sat up
and drank the dram of hot water,
kicked off the blankets,
lay there naked. I watched you breathing.
The lake was reflected on the ceiling:
a private aurora borealis as you slept.

I sit now in that room alone, a lung
where ghosts of us crust the air.
The room is heated and wooden geese
fly their migration frieze. They are to me
the things always leaving, a fever
that transforms in passing.
Now we're sick with distance,
that disease of spaces. I get better
slowly. It's odd what cured us then—
a little heat, a bit of company.

Casson

I remember how the blustery neighbour showed you off
like a big ring and left you on the dock
in a canvas chair with a ginger shandy
in your leathery hand. You were watching that island
just a short distance off across the water,

the water tacked down loose along the shore
like the skin of your face where your two dog-eyes
lay in deep blue mosaic. How's it going
I said, and you woke from your lake-dreaming life.
My wife, you said, she would have paddled me across

to Picnic Island and let me sleep in the stern.
But my knees are wrecked now—they go off
like rifles and I can't get into boats. It's fine
now (I suppose) to sit here and be among my friends.
Your hand pointed at the distant island. Then

the neighbour came and you held his hand and went
for your supper. His wife (whose body you imagined
in all its wild colours) propped you at the table head
and served you carrots and peas and potatoes and bread
which they ate with you in reverent silence.

Happy Hour

The chicken magnates sit
by the fireplace, spouting prices
in clipped dactyls, cigars glowing
like stars in the corner of the room.
Their wives circle the buffet,
loading up plates for them. Dogs
and children crowd underfoot, the din
is enormous. Outside,
incessant rain. Lake Nora is transfigured:
goose-flesh. All day my mother has prepared
for the gathering, poppy bagels, withered fish
with the eyes still in, a huge
anniversary cake.

Later, the grandparents stand
at the edge of the candles, chins glowing
and blow them out. A camera
grinds in someone's hands sucking up
the moment, freezing it in camera amber.
People navigate the thin hallway
to the bathroom, flat against the walls
like spies. A punch-line floats in the air
how should I know—I'm fourteen miles from home!
and my mother turns, laughing,
her mouth full of cake.

I look around. The chicken men are drunk,
their empty glasses tilt on their bellies.
A child has fallen asleep. A woman
I have never met thumbs up poppy seeds
from the table and eats them as she argues
with her neighbour. The crazy
aunt and uncle who still love each other
kiss in a corner. After this is all forgotten
we'll long for the background
where the unnamed visitor appears
in all the films, whose name
no one remembers. We'll watch those films
years from now, reviewing
the divorced and the dead,
that old ambient weather.
Someone will say, I wish I could go back
and someone else, No, never.

The nights were beautiful on the lake. There was a screen on the front porch to keep the mosquitoes out and we would sit there and watch the sky bruise. The men had their drinks, and the women sat closer to the screen, watching the water. Sometimes, a buzz from across the lake, a boat like a thought coming into someone's mind. Its red light floated over the surface far away from the sound of the engine. Across the lake, the skinny yellow fires lit by other families.

Sometimes Andy's parents would hold hands and sit so quietly for hours. One day long after all this, my mother went a little mad. My mother stopped believing my father's dreams would ever come true. She didn't know what to live for after that.

I can still see through that window, and feel the histories that lined the undercurrents of our lives. Nothing came to the surface, it skimmed along like the boat in the dark, in two parts, sound and vision. If we had all been lakes, we would have been deep with muddy beds. My mother would have been choppy waters, and my father, calm on the surface. Andy was an inlet, watching everything move past him. My two sisters, twin islands.

If I had been a lake, I would have flooded my shores.

At breakfast, my mother fried onions, green peppers and mushrooms in an electric skillet, a cigarette hanging over the mixture. Dad worked the juicer, skilfully slicing oranges in half and grinding the juice out. His was the domain of the finite recipe: ten oranges; five glasses of juice. Both families eventually made it downstairs in their housecoats while outside it rained, or the sun shined and the early birds were already out on boats and sailboards, and in the reeds that we could see from the front window two old men would be standing knee-deep, not catching anything, eating rice crackers and drinking coffee from silver canteens.

My sister Aimee liked to set the table, shuffling around in heavy slippers. Then the table laden with food: the vegetable compote, steaming and slick with butter, a plate of cold strawberries and melon, beef fry, pancakes with a dusting of sugar, fried eggs in pools of butter, their yellow suns quivering. Jams, marmalade, Marmite. Tea, Ovaltine, a white pot of coffee. Andy's dad wiping sleep from his eye.

If we had all been lakes, the sun would have filled our minds on mornings like that. My hands would have filled my plate with wind. Our bellies would have been clear and light, full of life, schools of fish, salamanders and frogs. Nothing would ever leave us empty. Our histories would float along with us. Nothing else would have to fill us.

The Return

Lake Nora has gone missing in her own body.
Submerged trees leave question marks
swirling in the water. From our canoe
we see filaments of decay hanging up
and the sun moving through them unchanged.
You call out your own name
and the shale walls send it back incomplete
as if woken from a dream. The quiet scares us—
we feel the loss of something unnamed,
like someone has sealed off the world below us.
I'm watching you, you're watching me.
It feels like one of us might disappear,
suddenly. Then something
leaves a rock and enters the lake—
all we can see is the echo spreading.
It comes out to touch the boat. *Stay with me.*

The Loon

It was dismantled like a machine
its brain exposed white as an egg
when we found it. Some twine
and a hook told part
of the story—a fishing accident
but could not explain
the further destruction.

Only last night, lying down with you
we'd heard its voice
slide over the lake
its rare blue sound like
the cry of a child
in nightmare. The bird's lonely
surprise, the nightly
realization of what it was.

But as that sound hooked
toward us in our secluded
dark, did we hear
its voice torn from it,
or its final warning
to boys in a boat
with their rods and knives,

their minds lulled
to killer bluntness by rum?

I am afraid, standing with you
here in the floating haze
above the ruined body
that it must have happened
after the cry we heard,
maybe immediately after,
and I had turned then
and put my mouth on your skin
and we had moved with
each other slowly, as if her
final cry described for us
the motion of our bodies.

But it was not until morning
that we crossed and found her here.

"Goodbye!"

I watch her go. Words seize in my throat. I turn and try to close the door, but the sky is bulging in the doorway. "I won't miss her," it says. The sky folds and unfolds a hanky in its hands. "I think I might cry all week." I bring the sky into the house. "I loved her as well," I say.

How long can I sit and not think of her?

I continue to live on the island. At night the stars lie in the lake: an underwater city. The lake becomes the sky—a lover watching a lover's face.

I sit at my table and the lake is my guest. On my plate is a salad of greens in balsamic vinegar. I have served the lake a few small stones. We sit and look into each other. We talk. This lake is deep! "You have to come by more often."

The lake flows down around the chair until her hair appears. The small stones become smooth as eyes and a tongue thickens in the air. Fingers lap onto the table.

The hair on my arms mats and thickens. My feet root in the floor, spreading out. Lines and grooves appear up my body. I long for wind. My eyes multiply in green and festoon the ends of my nerves, branching.

You're the one I love.

Two Meditations

i

A red-furred dog melts underground. A fine rain falls, soaking the soil. In puddles above the place it's buried, concentric eyes open over each other. Some of the dog rises up into the puddle and parts of the dog touch the air and slide in the water down to the lake. Then the dog becomes fish and lily-pad. On some mornings when it's very hot, the lake steams and some of the red-furred dog becomes air that rises and becomes part of a warm wall of air. Then it rains, a fine rain like hair.

ii

We're walking along with the field-guide, finding dogwood with its "head of small flowers." The book says nothing about its bark. I want to tell you about this place. I grew up here. Some years everything that lives vanishes from the lake, and in other years it's choked with fish. It's just inscrutable nature—not a mystical cycle. I can't stand those new religions—inventing magical order to stave off terror. If we let it happen, this place'll be overrun with suburban gurus quipping their monosyllabic negations. Sometimes when I walk here alone, I can't feel anything and I call that awestruck. I think that this place feels nothing for itself, not even *just is*. Ah—feel that? Look at that pool of water there: rain. O's opening—that's not awe, that's shock. OH. *So this is what I am.*

Last Picture of the Lake

The Arms is a box of windows and doors, a photo album
of discoloured squares, and Robbie is dead
at twenty-three, a scar-nest, a polished bone,
a fast dissolve to native shape,
a late vast travel to habitat.
And what is left I wander through—
this perishing picture, a closing iris
movie-view. The doomed bulk is eyeless
at lakeshore, unturreted, slack castle
dream-lacking and vanishing.
Yes I want to go back, but go back to what?
Now the sleeping rooms stretch their walls
in greens and browns, with bulging vines like fishing-lines
to a sky of residue—what's left is loam
a ship run aground,
a sound-chamber for the cries of loons,
a box for ghosts, an empty barn,
a little ark with darkened rooms.
Can you hear me still, my pirate,
across your kingdom of night-time blue?
Do you still slip and cut your feet on stones?
I want you to sleep in Lake Nora Arms.

Acknowledgements

I would like to thank the following people who read this book in manuscript form, for their generosity: Mary Cameron, Victor Coleman, Julia Dryer, Jeanne Iribarne, Patrick Lane, Mary Lindsay, Laura Lush, Don McKay, Michael Ondaatje, Linda Spalding and Eddy Yanofsky. Very special thanks to Steven Heighton and Albert Moritz. I wish also to acknowledge the support of the Ontario Arts Council.

The translator of the Pablo Neruda epigraph is Donald D. Walsh. The quote at the top of "Phases" (*"Ich glaube an Nächte"*—"I have faith in nights") is from the fifth poem of Rilke's great and early poem cycle *Das Stundenbuch* (*The Book of Hours*). The line *"I wish I could write a chapter upon sleep,"* in "Three Ships," is from *Tristram Shandy* by Laurence Sterne.

Some of these poems have appeared in *Brick, Poetry Canada Review, Quarry, The Apostle's Bar* and *Writ*. I thank the editors of those publications. "The Loon" first appeared in *Impromptu Feats of Balance* (Wolsak & Wynn, Don Mills, 1990).

This lake is a lake of fiction.

Toronto/Kingston/Gravenhurst
1987-1993